I0510117

THIS JOURNAL BELONGS TO

www.ingramcontent.com/pod-product-compliance
Lightning Source LLC
Chambersburg PA
CBHW030718220526
45463CB00005B/2105
* 9 7 8 1 6 9 0 1 3 1 0 4 5 *